How to Make a Camp

Written by Jillian Powell
Photographed by Tim Platt

Collins

Find a good place.

3

Tie a rope.

Peg a sheet.

Put some stones on the sheet.

Put a mat on the ground.

Have a picnic.

The camp

Ideas for reading

Written by Clare Dowdall, PhD
Lecturer and Primary Literacy Consultant

Reading objectives:
- read and understand simple sentences
- use phonic knowledge to decode regular words and read them aloud accurately
- demonstrate understanding when talking with others about what they have read

Communication and language objectives:
- develop their own narratives and explanations by connecting ideas or events
- listen to stories, accurately anticipating key events and respond to what they hear with relevant comments, questions or actions
- follow instructions involving several ideas or actions
- express themselves effectively, showing awareness of listeners' needs

Curriculum links: Understanding of the world

High frequency words: some, the, put

Interest words: camp, place, tie, rope, peg, sheet, stones, ground, picnic

Resources: whiteboard and pens, high frequency word cards, construction bricks and mini-figure toys

Word count: 18

Build a context for reading

- Ask children if they have ever made a tent or camp in their garden and to share their experiences. Explain that this book is an instruction book that tells you how to make a camp.

- Look at the front cover. Read the title and blurb together, pointing to the words as you read.

- Discuss why it is important to find a good place to make a camp. Ask children to suggest what a good place for building a camp would be like.

- Look at the high frequency words, using word cards. Help children to practise reading the words with digraphs, e.g. *place, tie, rope, sheet, ground.*

Understand and apply reading strategies

- Turn to pp2–3. Ask for a volunteer to read the text. Discuss what is happening in the pictures. Question the children to develop their ability to infer what is happening, e.g. *The children are pointing at two different trees. Maybe they will tie the rope to the trees.*

- Look at pp4–5. Ask for another volunteer to read the text. Support children to read the word *tie*, taking a cue from the pictures.